AMERICAN LEGENDS ALPHABET

Words by Robin Feiner

A is for **A**retha Franklin. Ranked by Rolling Stone as the No. 1 singer of all time, she earned the world's R-E-S-P-E-C-T by winning 18 Grammy Awards. Aretha was proudly the first woman to be inducted into the Rock & Roll Hall of Fame.

B is for Sitting **B**ull.
This Native American chief
led the Sioux tribes during
years of resistance against
United States policies.
Joining with Crazy Horse,
he famously defeated Custer
in the battle of Little Bighorn.

C is for **C**lint Eastwood. Famous for his roles in spaghetti Westerns, and as the infamous 'Dirty Harry,' Eastwood has become an enduring American icon of masculinity. Now on the other side of the camera, he is also a respected libertarian political figure.

D is for Dolly Parton. With nine Grammy Awards and 3000 songs to her name, Country music wouldn't sound as sweet if it weren't for this legendary singer-songwriter. She's also been working 9 to 5 helping kids to learn to read and write

E is for Eleanor Roosevelt. This first lady was outspoken and politically active about civil rights, women's rights and human rights, in general. She pressed America to join the UN, which saw her become known as 'First Lady of the World.'

F is for Frank Lloyd Wright. Inspired by nature, music, Japanese art and children's building blocks, Wright became the greatest American Architect of all time. Today, the original and innovative buildings he designed are considered national treasures.

G is for Matt **G**roening. From a rough sketch done minutes before the pitch, this quirky cartoonist created the longest running TV show in American history. Loved by kids and adults alike, 'The Simpsons' has even earned Matt a star on the Hollywood Walk of Fame. Ay caramba!

H is for **H**arriet Tubman. This legend escaped slavery, but returned a dozen times to free others. She led expeditions during the Civil War that liberated more than 700 slaves, and then went on to fight for women's rights. Harriet is an icon of American courage and freedom.

I is for Ira Glass.
This American Life, the show he hosts on National Public Radio, weaves storytelling, journalism, theatre and performance into unmissable weekly episodes. Ira is an inductee of the National Radio Hall of Fame and a true legend of the airwaves.

J is for Michael Jordan. 'Air Jordan' dazzled crowds with his prolific scoring, incredible defense, and famous gravity-defying slam dunks. He is without question the greatest b-baller of all time, possessing enough star power to globalize the sport.

K is for Martin Luther **K**ing Jr. Taking the reins of the Civil Rights Movement, King fought peacefully for an end to racial inequality. As well as winning the Nobel Peace Prize, he and his dream are remembered with a national holiday.

L is for Abraham Lincoln. 'Honest Abe' led the United States through its greatest crisis, the American Civil War. For abolishing slavery, preserving the Union, and for his legendary Gettysburg Address, he is considered the greatest U.S. president of all time.

M is for **M**uhammad Ali. Born Cassius Clay but known as 'the Greatest,' this champion boxer beat everyone who dared take him on. Ali wasn't just a 'Thrilla' in the ring ... this legend was also a knock out for the Civil Rights Movement.

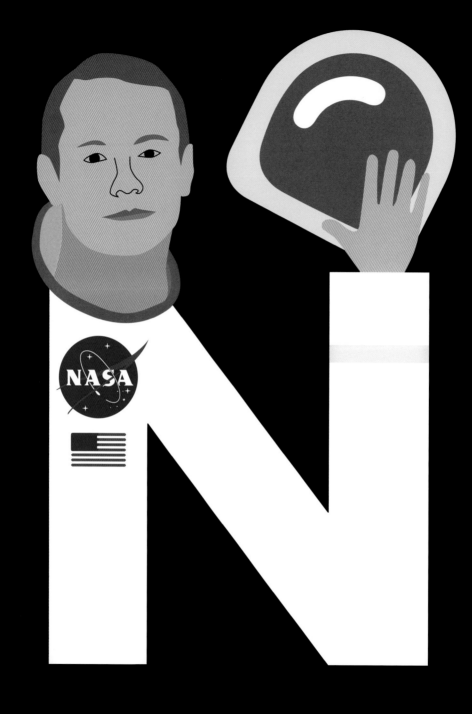

N is for Neil Armstrong.
In 1969, he helped mankind take one giant leap forward when, as a NASA astronaut, he bravely became the first man to step foot on the Moon. Awarded the Presidential Medal of Freedom, this legend will be forever celebrated.

O is for Oprah Winfrey. With charisma, empathy and wisdom in spades, she has become a personality with unprecedented popularity and influence. The 'Queen of All Media' is an inspiration to women from all backgrounds.

P is for Elvis Presley. Known as the 'King of Rock and Roll,' or 'The King' to his true fans, Elvis is one of the most significant cultural icons of the 20th century. With a voice and moves that made women swoon, he won hearts the world over.

Q is for Steve McQueen. Known as 'The King of Cool,' the rebellious McQueen became a huge box-office hit of the 60s and 70s. With an obsession for motor-racing, he would perform his own stunts magnificently.

R is for Wilma **R**udolph. This world record holding Olympic legend from Clarkesville, Tennessee, was considered the fastest woman in the world, and one of the most famous. She was a further inspiration as a civil rights and women's rights pioneer.

S is for Steve Jobs.
With an inspiring vision
for computers that were
useful, friendly and stylish,
Jobs co-founded Apple.
Now the most valuable
company in the history
of the world, it's hard to
imagine life without his
marvelous inventions.

T is for Mark **T**wain. Credited with writing the 'Great American Novel,' the 'Father of American literature's,' humorous stories were adored by all. His legendary adventure stories, featuring Huckleberry Finn and Tom Sawyer, are a must read.

U is for **U**lysses S. Grant. This military genius was appointed by Lincoln to lead the Union Army to victory over the Confederacy in the American Civil War. He then went on to lead the nation as its 18th Commander-in-Chief.

V is **V**ictoria Woodhull. She was a bold pioneer who famously fought for women's rights as leader of the suffrage movement. She was the first woman to run for President, open a firm on Wall Street, and start a newspaper as well. Legend!

W is for Andy **W**arhol. As a pioneer of the Pop Art movement, Warhol created some of the most iconic, memorable and collectible American artworks of the 20th century. In fact, the largest personal museum in the U.S. is dedicated to this legend and his art.

X is for Malcolm **X.** Known as one of the most influential African Americans in history, Malcolm was a fierce and courageous advocate for the rights of blacks. He famously led the 1963 Unity Rally in Harlem, and inspired thousands with his stirring speeches.

Yy

Y is for **Yo-Yo Ma.** This child prodigy was performing at the age of four. He now plays with orchestras around the world, has won 18 Grammy Awards, has recorded over 90 albums, and plays a cello worth 2.5 million dollars.

Z is for Ground **Z**ero.
All the incredibly brave
fire-fighters, police officers,
paramedics and others
who, as first responders,
gave of themselves so
selflessly on the 11th of
September 2001, we salute
you. It's legends like you who
truly make America great.